12,000

DREAMS
interpreted

JOURNAL

12,000

DREAMS
interpreted
JOURNAL

GUSTAVUS HINDMAN MILLER

REVISED AND REINTERPRETED BY

Linda Shields AND **Lenore Skomal**

STERLING ETHOS
New York

STERLING ETHOS

New York

An Imprint of Sterling Publishing
387 Park Avenue South
New York, NY 10016

ISBN 978-1-4549-1337-5

Distributed in Canada by Sterling Publishing
℅ Canadian Manda Group, 165 Dufferin Street
Toronto, Ontario, Canada M6K 3H6
Distributed in the United Kingdom by GMC Distribution Services
Castle Place, 166 High Street, Lewes, East Sussex, England BN7 1XU
Distributed in Australia by Capricorn Link (Australia) Pty. Ltd.
P.O. Box 704, Windsor, NSW 2756, Australia

For information about custom editions, special sales, and premium
and corporate purchases, please contact Sterling Special Sales at 800-805-5489
or specialsales@sterlingpublishing.com.

Manufactured in the United States of America

2 4 6 8 10 9 7 5 3 1

www.sterlingpublishing.com

INTRODUCTION

*W*hat is a dream? Is it somewhere we go to escape life's ups and downs? Is it a prophecy of what is to come in the future? Or perhaps a message from the past, a long-deceased loved one reaching out from the misty depths of the spirit world? Or could it be the spirit world trying to warn or tell us something that we need at that moment for clarity? Might it be our subconscious mind, clarifying a problem in our life or giving us a glimpse of future events to come? Or is it simply that pickle we ate before bed? The answer to all these questions is "yes." For most of us, dreams materialize in the form of a story. And, as with any story, there are components that together make up the whole, whether or not they make sense individually. That's where this book comes in.

We suggest you keep this journal by your bed so that you can make a list of all the elements of your dream immediately upon waking. Dreams are quick to flee from the memory, and every element of a dream can add to its successful interpretation. Write as much down as you can remember. Once you are finished, you can uncover the real meaning of the words or elements using the dictionary in the back of this book. It contains some of the most commonly-seen dream symbols selected from the full 12,000 available in *12,000 Dreams Interpreted*.

With a little practice, interpreting a dream can be easy and enjoyable. We hope this journal gives you a place to record your dreams, helping you to unlock their hidden meanings and understand the true messages of your subconscious.

———— * ———— * ————

☾ *Tonight I dreamed . . .*

_____ * _____ * _____

🌙 *Tonight I dreamed . . .*

_____ * _____ * _____

 *Tonight I dreamed . . .*

_____ * _____ * _____

☾ *Tonight I dreamed . . .*

_____ ✳ _____ ✳ _____

🌙 *Tonight I dreamed . . .*

———— * ———— * ————

☾ *Tonight I dreamed . . .*

____ * ____ * ____

Tonight I dreamed . . .

_____ * _____ * _____

🌙 *Tonight I dreamed . . .*

_____ * _____ * _____

☾ Tonight I dreamed . . .

"*There is nothing like dreams to create the future. Utopia today, flesh and blood tomorrow.*"

—**Victor Hugo** (1802-1885)

___ * ___ * ___

☾ *Tonight I dreamed . . .*

_____ * _____ * _____

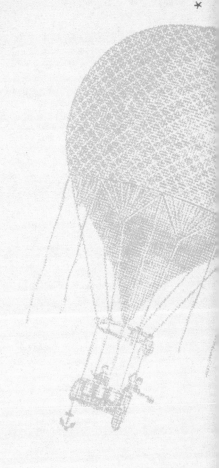 *Tonight I dreamed . . .*

___ * ___ * ___

☾ *Tonight I dreamed . . .*

———— * ———— * ————

🌙 *Tonight I dreamed . . .*

———— ✳ ———— ✳ ————

 ☾ *Tonight I dreamed . . .*

_____ * _____ * _____

🌙 *Tonight I dreamed . . .*

_____ * _____ * _____

Tonight I dreamed . . .

_____ * _____ * _____

☾ *Tonight I dreamed . . .*

_____ * _____ * _____

🌙 *Tonight I dreamed . . .*

——— * ——— * ———

🌙 *Tonight I dreamed . . .*

——— * ——— * ———

🌙 *Tonight I dreamed . . .*

"If you will it,
it is no dream."

—Theodor Herzl (1860-1904)

———— * ———— * ————

☾ *Tonight I dreamed . . .*

——— * ——— * ———

🌙 *Tonight I dreamed . . .*

_____ * _____ * _____

☾ *Tonight I dreamed . . .*

—— * —— * ——

🌙 *Tonight I dreamed . . .*

—— * —— * ——

Tonight I dreamed . . .

——— * ——— * ———

🌙 *Tonight I dreamed . . .*

_____ ✳ _____ ✳ _____

🌙 *Tonight I dreamed . . .*

_____ * _____ * _____

☾ *Tonight I dreamed . . .*

———— * ———— * ————

☾ *Tonight I dreamed . . .*

"Dream no small dreams for they have no power to move the hearts of men."
—Johann Wolfgang von Goethe (1749-1832)

—— * —— * ——

 *Tonight I dreamed ...*

———— * ———— * ————

☾ *Tonight I dreamed . . .*

_____ * _____ * _____

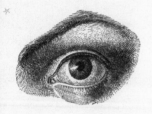 ☾ *Tonight I dreamed . . .*

——— * ——— * ———

☾ *Tonight I dreamed . . .*

_____ * _____ * _____

🌙 *Tonight I dreamed . . .*

_____ * _____ * _____

🌙 *Tonight I dreamed . . .*

——— ✳ ——— ✳ ———

🌙 *Tonight I dreamed . . .*

_____ * _____ * _____

 *Tonight I dreamed . . .*

"It may be that those who do most, dream most."

—Stephen Butler Leacock (1869-1944)

_____ * _____ * _____

🌙 *Tonight I dreamed . . .*

_____ * _____ * _____

☾ *Tonight I dreamed . . .*

_____ * _____ * _____

Tonight I dreamed . . .

Tonight I dreamed . . .

_____ * _____ * _____

☾ *Tonight I dreamed . . .*

———— * ———— * ————

☾ *Tonight I dreamed . . .*

_____ * _____ * _____

🌙 *Tonight I dreamed . . .*

———— * ———— * ————

☾ *Tonight I dreamed . . .*

____ * ____ * ____

 *Tonight I dreamed . . .*

"The center of every man's existence is a dream."

—G.K. Chesterton (1874-1936)

—— * —— * ——

🌙 *Tonight I dreamed . . .*

_____ * _____ * _____

🌙 *Tonight I dreamed . . .*

———— * ———— * ————

🌙 *Tonight I dreamed . . .*

——— * ——— * ———

Tonight I dreamed . . .

_____ * _____ * _____

🌙 *Tonight I dreamed . . .*

———— * ———— * ————

🌙 *Tonight I dreamed . . .*

_____ * _____ * _____

☾ *Tonight I dreamed . . .*

—— ＊ —— ＊ ——

🌙 *Tonight I dreamed . . .*

—— * —— * ——

☾ *Tonight I dreamed . . .*

"Each man should frame life so that at some
future hour fact and his dreaming meet."

—Victor Hugo (1802-1885)

_____ * _____ * _____

🌙 *Tonight I dreamed . . .*

———— * ———— * ————

☾ *Tonight I dreamed . . .*

☾ *Tonight I dreamed . . .*

_____ * _____ * _____

☾ *Tonight I dreamed . . .*

_____ * _____ * _____

 ☾ *Tonight I dreamed . . .*

——— * ——— * ———

🌙 *Tonight I dreamed . . .*

_____ ✳ _____ ✳ _____

☾ *Tonight I dreamed . . .*

_____ * _____ * _____

🌙 *Tonight I dreamed . . .*

_____ * _____ * _____

🌙 *Tonight I dreamed . . .*

_____ ✳ _____ ✳ _____

☾ *Tonight I dreamed . . .*

——— * ——— * ———

☾ *Tonight I dreamed . . .*

"Keep true to
the dreams of
thy youth."

—Friedrich von Schiller (1759-1805)

_____ * _____ * _____

☽ *Tonight I dreamed . . .*

_____ * _____ * _____

🌙 *Tonight I dreamed . . .*

———— * ———— * ————

🌙 *Tonight I dreamed . . .*

_____ * _____ * _____

🌙 *Tonight I dreamed . . .*

_____ * _____ * _____

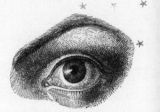 *Tonight I dreamed . . .*

_____ * _____ * _____

 *Tonight I dreamed ...*

"*Dreams are often most profound when they seem the most crazy.*"

—**Sigmund Freud** (1856-1939)

———— * ———— * ————

🌙 *Tonight I dreamed . . .*

——— * ——— * ———

☾ Tonight I dreamed . . .

_____ * _____ * _____

 *Tonight I dreamed . . .*

———— ✳ ———— ✳ ————

☾ *Tonight I dreamed . . .*

___ * ___ * ___

Tonight I dreamed . . .

_____ * _____ * _____

🌙 *Tonight I dreamed . . .*

_____ * _____ * _____

🌙 *Tonight I dreamed . . .*

_____ * _____ * _____

 *Tonight I dreamed . . .*

____ * ____ * ____

🌙 *Tonight I dreamed . . .*

—— ✳ —— ✳ ——

🌙 *Tonight I dreamed . . .*

"*Dreaming is an act of pure imagination, attesting in all men a creative power, which if it were available in waking, would make every man a Dante or Shakespeare*"

—Fredrick Henry Hedge (1805-1890)

_____ ✳ _____ ✳ _____

🌙 *Tonight I dreamed . . .*

_____ * _____ * _____

 *Tonight I dreamed . . .*

_____ * _____ * _____

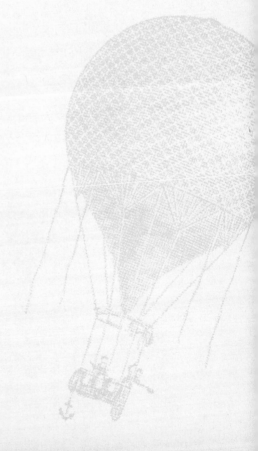

🌙 *Tonight I dreamed . . .*

_____ * _____ * _____

🌙 *Tonight I dreamed . . .*

_____ ∗ _____ ∗ _____

☾ *Tonight I dreamed . . .*

Tonight I dreamed . . .

_____ ✳ _____ ✳ _____

🌙 *Tonight I dreamed . . .*

——— ✳ ——— ✳ ———

🌙 *Tonight I dreamed . . .*

———— * ———— * ————

☾ *Tonight I dreamed ...*

_____ * _____ * _____

🌙 *Tonight I dreamed . . .*

"*The wisest men follow their own direction.*"

—Euripides (480 BC-406 BC)

_____ * _____ * _____

☾ *Tonight I dreamed . . .*

_____ * _____ * _____

☾ *Tonight I dreamed ...*

___ * ___ * ___

☾ *Tonight I dreamed . . .*

—— * —— * ——

Tonight I dreamed . . .

———— * ———— * ————

Tonight I dreamed . . .

———— * ———— * ————

🌙 *Tonight I dreamed . . .*

____ * ____ * ____

🌙 *Tonight I dreamed . . .*

—— * —— * ——

🌙 *Tonight I dreamed . . .*

____ * ____ * ____

Tonight I dreamed . . .

_____ ✳ _____ ✳ _____

🌙 *Tonight I dreamed . . .*

"*A dream which is not interpreted is like a letter which is not read..*"

—The Talmud

——— ✳ ——— ✳ ———

🌙 *Tonight I dreamed . . .*

_____ * _____ * _____

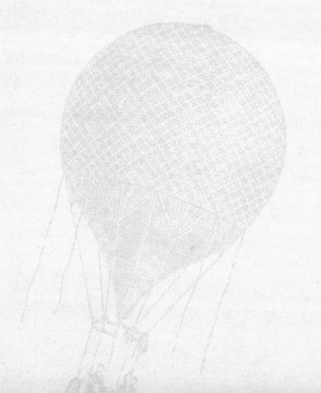 *Tonight I dreamed . . .*

_____ * _____ * _____

🌙 *Tonight I dreamed . . .*

Tonight I dreamed . . .

_____ * _____ * _____

Tonight I dreamed . . .

___ * ___ * ___

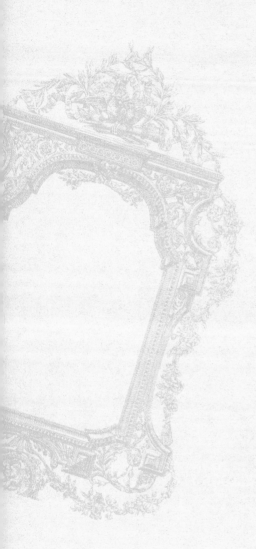 ☾ *Tonight I dreamed . . .*

_____ * _____ * _____

☾ *Tonight I dreamed . . .*

———— ✳ ———— ✳ ————

☾ *Tonight I dreamed . . .*

——— ✳ ——— ✳ ———

🌙 *Tonight I dreamed . . .*

———— ✳ ———— ✳ ————

🌙 *Tonight I dreamed . . .*

———— ✳ ———— ✳ ————

🌙 *Tonight I dreamed . . .*

*"To accomplish great things, we must not only act,
but also dream; not only plan, but also believe."*
—Anatole France (1844-1924)

——— * ——— * ———

Tonight I dreamed . . .

_____ * _____ * _____

Tonight I dreamed . . .

_____ * _____ * _____

🌙 *Tonight I dreamed . . .*

_____ * _____ * _____

 Tonight I dreamed . . .

———— ✳ ———— ✳ ————

🌙 *Tonight I dreamed . . .*

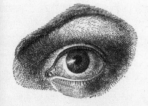

____ * ____ * ____

🌙 *Tonight I dreamed . . .*

_____ * _____ * _____

🌙 *Tonight I dreamed . . .*

_____ ✻ _____ ✻ _____

🌙 *Tonight I dreamed . . .*

☾ *Tonight I dreamed . . .*

_____ * _____ * _____

☾ *Tonight I dreamed . . .*

"All men who have achieved great things have been great dreamers."

—**Orison Swett Marden** (1850-1924)

——— * ——— * ———

🌙 *Tonight I dreamed . . .*

——— * ——— * ———

🌙 *Tonight I dreamed . . .*

_____ * _____ * _____

Tonight I dreamed . . .

———— ✳ ———— ✳ ————

 *Tonight I dreamed . . .*

_____ * _____ * _____

🌙 *Tonight I dreamed . . .*

_____ * _____ * _____

🌙 *Tonight I dreamed . . .*

_____ * _____ * _____

Tonight I dreamed . . .

──── ✳ ──── ✳ ────

🌙 *Tonight I dreamed . . .*

_____ * _____ * _____

🌙 *Tonight I dreamed . . .*

___ * ___ * ___

🌙 *Tonight I dreamed . . .*

"Don't be pushed by your problems. Be led by your dreams."

—Ralph Waldo Emerson (1803-1882)

_____ * _____ * _____

🌙 *Tonight I dreamed . . .*

———— * ———— * ————

☾ *Tonight I dreamed . . .*

_____ * _____ * _____

 *Tonight I dreamed ...*

_____ * _____ * _____

🌙 *Tonight I dreamed . . .*

——— * ——— * ———

☾ Tonight I dreamed . . .

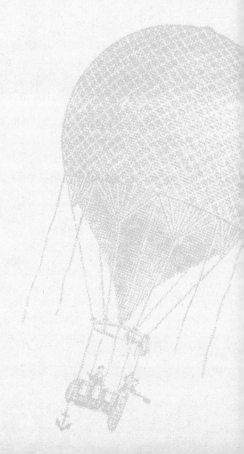

_____ * _____ * _____

🌙 *Tonight I dreamed . . .*

___ * ___ * ___

🌙 *Tonight I dreamed . . .*

_____ * _____ * _____

☾ *Tonight I dreamed . . .*

_____ * _____ * _____

🌙 *Tonight I dreamed . . .*

———— * ———— * ————

☾ *Tonight I dreamed . . .*

———— ＊ ———— ＊ ————

🌙 *Tonight I dreamed . . .*

"A man is not old until regrets take the place of dreams."
—John Barrymore (1882-1942)

_____ * _____ * _____

Tonight I dreamed . . .

———— * ———— * ————

🌙 *Tonight I dreamed . . .*

———— * ———— * ————

☾ *Tonight I dreamed . . .*

____ * ____ * ____

 *Tonight I dreamed . . .*

___ * ___ * ___

🌙 *Tonight I dreamed . . .*

—— * —— * ——

☾ *Tonight I dreamed . . .*

_____ * _____ * _____

☾ *Tonight I dreamed . . .*

———— * ———— * ————

☾ *Tonight I dreamed . . .*

_____ * _____ * _____

🌙 *Tonight I dreamed . . .*

_____ * _____ * _____

🌙 *Tonight I dreamed . . .*

"*Trust in dreams, for in them is the hidden gate to eternity..*"

—**Khalil Gibran** (1883-1931)

____ * ____ * ____

☾ *Tonight I dreamed . . .*

_____ * _____ * _____

☾ *Tonight I dreamed . . .*

4

_____ * _____ * _____

☾ *Tonight I dreamed . . .*

———— * ———— * ————

☾ *Tonight I dreamed* . . .

＿＿＿ ＊ ＿＿＿ ＊ ＿＿＿

☾ *Tonight I dreamed . . .*

C Tonight I dreamed . . .

____ * ____ * ____

☾ *Tonight I dreamed . . .*

_____ * _____ * _____

🌙 *Tonight I dreamed . . .*

_____ * _____ * _____

Tonight I dreamed . . .

_____ * _____ * _____

🌙 *Tonight I dreamed . . .*

🌙 *Tonight I dreamed . . .*

"*Every great dream begins with a dreamer.*"

—Harriet Tubman (1822-1913)

_____ * _____ * _____

☾ *Tonight I dreamed . . .*

_____ * _____ * _____

Tonight I dreamed . . .

———— ＊ ———— ＊ ————

☾ *Tonight I dreamed . . .*

_____ * _____ * _____

☾ *Tonight I dreamed . . .*

_____ * _____ * _____

🌙 *Tonight I dreamed . . .*

☽ *Tonight I dreamed . . .*

_____ * _____ * _____

🌙 *Tonight I dreamed . . .*

———— * ———— * ————

☾ *Tonight I dreamed . . .*

———— * ———— * ————

🌙 *Tonight I dreamed . . .*

_____ ✳ _____ ✳ _____

🌙 *Tonight I dreamed . . .*

_____ * _____ * _____

🌙 *Tonight I dreamed . . .*

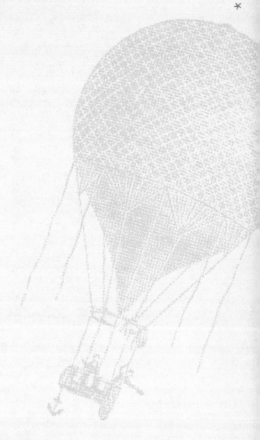

_____ ✳ _____ ✳ _____

☾ *Tonight I dreamed . . .*

——— * ——— * ———

☾ *Tonight I dreamed . . .*

"I have spread my dreams beneath your feet.
Tread softly because you tread on my dreams."

—W.B Yeats (1865-1939)

☾ *Tonight I dreamed . . .*

_____ * _____ * _____

Tonight I dreamed . . .

—— * —— * ——

🌙 *Tonight I dreamed . . .*

_____ * _____ * _____

☾ *Tonight I dreamed . . .*

___ * ___ * ___

☾ *Tonight I dreamed . . .*

_____ * _____ * _____

Tonight I dreamed ...

_____ * _____ * _____

🌙 *Tonight I dreamed . . .*

"*Whatever you can do, or dream you can, begin it.*"

— *Attributed to* **Johann Wolfgang von Goethe** (1749-1832)

ABDUCTION

To be abducted or kidnapped in a dream is a warning that you must leave a situation in your life that no longer serves you, and you should do so regardless of your desires at this time.

ADAM AND EVE

To dream of Adam and Eve tells you that many blessings are coming your way.

ADULTERY

To dream of committing adultery foretells that you will be arraigned for some illegal action or will be embarrassed socially.

AFTERNOON

To dream of a sunny afternoon corresponds to friendships that are lasting and entertaining. A cloudy, rainy afternoon implies disappointment and displeasure.

AUGUST

In dreams, the month of August represents unfortunate deals and misunderstandings in love affairs.

AUTOPSY

To dream of conducting an autopsy or of watching one means that you need to examine, dissect, and cut out those parts of your life that no longer serve you.

AWKWARDNESS

To feel awkward in a situation or around a person means the opposite: you will have all the courage and confidence you need to face something that previously daunted you.

BABY

To dream of crying babies is indicative of ill health and disappointments. A happy baby denotes love requited and many warm friends.

BACON

It is good to dream of eating bacon.

BAGEL

If you dream of eating a bagel or making one, expect to go around in circles before you find a solution to a problem—but you will find one.

BALDNESS

If you see a bald person in a dream, expect a change that will benefit you.

BANK

To see an empty bank in a dream foretells of business losses. Giving out money denotes carelessness; receiving it, great gain and prosperity.

BAPTISM

To dream of baptism advises you to strengthen your character by showing restraint when offering your opinions. To dream that you are being baptized signifies that you will humiliate your inner self for public favor.

BAR, BARTENDING

To dream of tending a bar warns that you may resort to some questionable mode of advancement. Seeing a bar denotes community activity, quick improvement of finances, or the consummation of illicit desires.

BASKETBALL

To participate in this sport in your dream means you will reach your goals. To be a spectator watching a basketball game in your dream advises you to stop sitting on the sidelines in your waking life and participate more fully.

BATHROOM

To dream of a bathroom is an omen of good luck.

BEARD

To dream of seeing a beard suggests that an uncongenial person will oppose you. You may experience a fierce struggle for mastery and you are likely to lose money. A gray beard signifies hard luck and quarrels. To see a beard on a woman foretells unpleasant associations and lingering illness.

BED

Dreaming of a bed, clean and white, denotes peace of mind. To dream of making a bed signifies a new friendship or business associate.

BELLS

To hear bells tolling in your dreams means death.

BERRIES

To dream of berries on the vine, or of eating them, means that you have good social standing among your peers. This also signals material wealth and good fortune.

BIBLE

To dream of the Bible indicates blessings and good fortune.

BIRTHDAY

To the young, to dream of a birthday is a signal of poverty and falsehood. To the old, it indicates long trouble and desolation.

BLINDNESS

To dream of being blind denotes a sudden change from affluence to poverty. To see others blind means that a worthy person will call on you for aid.

BRAIN

To see your own brain in a dream warns that uncongenial surroundings will turn you into an unpleasant companion.

CALORIES

If you dream of calories, you are being warned to watch your eating habits, which might lead to health issues.

CANCER

If you dream of having cancer, have faith that you will be happy. To dream that someone else has cancer means you will bring happiness to someone in the very near future

CANNIBAL

If you dream of a cannibal or a tribe of cannibals, take care to avoid being taken advantage of in a business deal.

CAR

To dream of seeing cars denotes journeys and changes in quick succession. To get into one shows that the travel you've been contemplating will be made under circumstances different from what you thought.

CARNIVAL

To dream that you are participating in a carnival portends that you are soon to enjoy some unusual pleasure or recreation. If masks are in use, or you see incongruous or clownish figures, expect discord in the home; business will be unsatisfactory and love unrequited.

CASTLE

If you dream of being in a castle, you have enough money to make the life you wish to live. You can be a great traveler, enjoying contact with people of many nations.

CAVITY

To dream of having a cavity means you will soon have a wish fulfilled.

CELL PHONE

To dream of a cell phone with good reception indicates clear thinking about a project. If it has poor reception, you might be confused by other people's ideas.

CHEATING

If you dream of being cheated in business, you will meet designing people who seek to close your avenues to fortune.

CHILDBIRTH

To dream of giving birth predicts fortunate circumstances and the safe delivery of a beautiful baby. For an unmarried woman to dream of being in childbirth denotes unhappy changes from honor to disgrace.

CHRISTMAS TREE

To dream of a Christmas tree denotes joyful occasions and an auspicious fortune. To see one dismantled foretells that a painful incident will follow a festive occasion.

COCAINE

To dream of being addicted to cocaine or to use it means sorrow is coming your way.

CONDOM

To use or wear a condom in your dreams means you will soon need to pay close attention to business dealings.

CONTACT LENS

To lose a contact lens in your dream recommends that you open your eyes to deception.

COUGHING

To dream that you are aggravated by a constant cough indicates poor health; but you will recuperate if you take care and exercise good habits

CRUCIFIX

To see a crucifix in a dream is a good omen and a blessing.

DANCING

To the married, to dream of seeing a crowd of merry children dancing signifies loving, obedient, and intelligent children and a cheerful and comfortable home. To young people, it denotes easy tasks and many pleasures.

DAUGHTER

To dream of your daughter suggests that displeasing incidents will give way to pleasure and harmony. If in the dream she disappoints you for any reason, you will suffer vexation and discontent.

DEAD

To dream of the dead means rebirth and new beginnings.

DEMOCRAT

To dream of being a Democrat when you are not means you will be seeking advice from someone you never thought you would look to for help.

DEMON

To be in the presence of a demon in your dream warns you of evil doings around you. To fight and defeat a demon suggests that you will have many blessings in family, home, and work.

DEODORANT

To dream that you need to put this on means good health. To refuse to wear it in your dream means you will soon have a health problem that needs immediate attention.

DESSERT

To dream that you are eating dessert is a good omen, unless you're eating it alone; then it warns of the ending of a friendship. To make or bake a dessert means good luck.

DIAMOND

To dream of owning diamonds is a very propitious dream, signifying great honor and recognition from high places.

DINNER

To dream of eating dinner alone indicates that you will often have cause to think seriously of the necessities of life.

DISCOVERY

To dream you make a discovery of any kind means you will soon lose a treasured item. This warning dream reminds you to be careful of your things.

DIVING

To dream of diving into clear water signifies a favorable end to some embarrassment. If the water is muddy, you will suffer anxiety at the turn your affairs seem to be taking.

DOCTOR

It is a most auspicious dream, denoting good health and general prosperity, if you meet a doctor socially, for you will not then spend your money on his or her services.

DOG

To dream of a vicious dog suggests enemies and unalterable misfortune. To dream that a dog nuzzles you indicates great gain and constant friends. A dog with fine qualities lets you know that you will be possessed of solid wealth.

DOLL

To dream of a doll suggests social and familial happiness.

DOVE

Dreaming of doves mating and building their nests indicates a peaceful world and joyous homes where children are obedient and mercy is extended to all.

DRY CLEANING

To dream of bringing clothing to a dry cleaner means you will soon be "cleaning" up past relationships that have ended. To pick up items from the dry cleaner in your dream suggests that new friendships are coming your way.

EAR

If you dream of seeing ears, an evil and designing person is keeping watch over your conversation to harm you.

ECLIPSE

To dream of an eclipse of the sun denotes temporary failure in business and other affairs, as well as disturbances in families. An eclipse of the moon foretells contagious disease or death.

EGG

To dream of finding a nest of eggs denotes wealth of a substantial character, and happiness and many children among the married. To eat eggs implies that unusual disturbances threaten you in your home

ELEVATOR

To dream of ascending in an elevator means that you will swiftly rise to position and wealth; but if you descend in one, your misfortunes will crush and discourage you. If you see one descending without you, you will narrowly escape disappointment in some undertaking.

EXAM

To dream of taking an exam and failing suggests that you are aiming too high; there is something you probably won't be able to accomplish.

FACES

This dream is favorable if you see happy and bright faces, but it signifies trouble if they are disfigured, ugly, or frowning at you. To a young person, an ugly face foretells lovers' quarrels; or for a lover to see the face of his or her sweetheart looking old warns of separation and the breakup of happy associations.

FALLING

To dream that you sustain a fall and are frightened means that you will undergo some great struggle but will eventually rise to honor and wealth. If you are injured in the fall, you will encounter hardships and loss of friends.

FATHER

To dream of your father signifies that you are about to be involved in a difficulty and will need wise counsel if you hope to extricate yourself. If your father is dead, the dream suggests that your business is affecting you negatively; you will have to use caution in conducting it.

FEAR

To dream that you feel fear, from any cause, suggests that your future engagements will not prove as successful as you expect.

FINGERS

To dream of seeing your fingers scratched and bleeding implies much trouble and suffering. You will despair of making your way through life. Beautiful hands with clean fingers suggest that your love will be requited and that you will become renowned for your benevolence.

FLIES

In dreams, flies represent sickness and contagious maladies. They also indicate that enemies surround you.

FOOD

Eating fresh food in a dream is a sign of good luck. Dreaming of eating spoiled or rotting food warns you to expect setbacks in something you are planning. Selling food in a dream means good monetary luck, while buying it signifies a happy family celebration on the horizon.

FUNERAL

To see a funeral in your dream denotes an unhappy marriage and sickly offspring. If this is the funeral of a stranger, it suggests unexpected worries. If it's your child's, it may denote health among your family, or it may suggest very grave disappointments from a friendly source. To dream of the funeral of any relative implies psychological or emotional issues and family worries.

FUTURE

To dream of the future suggests careful reckoning and avoidance of detrimental extravagance.

GAMBLING

To dream that you are gambling and win suggests low associations and pleasure at the expense of others. If you lose, it foretells that your disgraceful conduct will be the undoing of someone near you.

GANG

To dream of being in a gang means that you are not taking a leadership role in your relationships. Being afraid of or threatened by a gang in your dream suggests that you're in a time of depression that only you can overcome.

GARBAGE

To see heaps of garbage in your dream indicates thoughts of social scandal and unfavorable business of all kinds.

GARDEN

To dream of a garden filled with evergreens and flowers denotes great peace of mind and comfort. Vegetables in a garden suggest misery or calumny and loss of fortune.

GAS

To dream of gas implies that you entertain harmful opinions of others and deal with them unjustly, and then suffer consequent remorse. To think you are asphyxiated in a dream indicates that you will incur trouble through your own wastefulness and negligence.

GENITALS

To dream of healthy genitals, either male or female, means a good love life is in the future. If the genitals in your dream are diseased or deformed, however, the dream is warning that you are being too forward and possibly promiscuous in your sex life.

GERMS

To see, be aware of, or worry about germs in a dream foretells the renewal of energy and vitality in your life.

GUILT

To dream of others being guilty means that some of your friends are untrustworthy. Be careful. To dream of feeling guilty predicts renewed friendships.

HAIR

To see your hair turning gray foretells death and contagion in the family of some relative or friend. To see yourself covered with hair is an omen of indulgence in vices to an extent that will disbar you from the society of refined people. If you see well-kept and neatly combed hair, your fortune will improve.

HALLOWEEN

In dreams, this holiday represents recognition in community affairs.

HANDCUFFS

Finding yourself handcuffed in your dreams means that you will be annoyed and vexed by enemies. You may also be menaced with sickness and danger. To see others thus means that you will subdue those oppressing you and rise above your associates.

HANDICAP

To dream of being handicapped indicates good health. To dream of seeing someone else handicapped warns you to see your doctor soon. Helping a handicapped person—or being helped if you are handicapped—suggests that dealing with a health issue will have an excellent outcome.

HANGOVER

To dream that you are experiencing a hangover, if you are single, warns against being morally loose and promiscuous. For a married person to dream of being hungover implies a release from familial problems.

HDTV

Dreaming of watching a program in HDTV means you will find yourself balanced in your emotional life.

HEAT WAVE

To dream of a heat wave indicates that a financial problem is on the horizon due to a mechanical problem or breakdown out of your control.

HIV

To dream that you have this disease foretells good news about a current health issue. But if you dream of someone else having HIV, you may have a health problem that shouldn't be ignored.

HOLY LAND

If you dream of being in the Holy Land or taking a trip to the Holy Land, extraordinary blessings are coming your way.

HOMOSEXUALITY

To dream you are homosexual when you are not means that your love is pure and well intentioned.

HUSBAND

If you dream that your husband is leaving you, and you do not understand why, there will be bitterness between you, but an unexpected reconciliation will follow. If he mistreats you and upbraids you for unfaithfulness, you will have his regard and confidence, but other worries will ensue; you are warned to be more discreet in receiving attention from men. If you see him dead, disappointment and sorrow will envelop you.

ICE CREAM

To dream that you are eating ice cream foretells success in affairs already undertaken. To see children eating it suggests that prosperity and happiness will attend you most favorably. If it is melted, though, your anticipated pleasure will stagnate before you can realize it.

IMPLANT

To dream of having an implant in your body betokens good health, social rewards, and financial gain.

INCEST

To dream of incestuous practices means that you will fall from honorable places and will also suffer loss in business.

INFANT

To dream of seeing a newborn infant suggests that pleasant surprises are nearing you.

INJECTION

To dream you are injecting something into yourself or someone else warns against upcoming health issues.

IN-LAWS

To dream of your in-laws foretells family harmony. To dream that you are an in-law means that a family problem is on the horizon.

INTERNET

To dream that you are trying to connect to the Internet and cannot indicates that you have trouble getting your ideas across in a project at work. To be able to connect predicts that you will have an easy time in the same project.

INTERVIEW

To dream of preparing for, or going on, an interview foretells the coming of money. To dream that you are being interviewed and do not get the job implies a small financial loss that you'll soon recover from. To dream that you do get the job means a surprise gift or unexpected monetary gain in the near future.

ISLAND

To dream that you are on an island in a clear stream signifies pleasant journeys and fortunate enterprises. A barren island indicates forfeiture of happiness and money through intemperance.

JAIL

If you dream of being confined in jail, you will be prevented from doing profitable work by the intervention of envious people; if you escape, however, you will enjoy a season of favorable business.

JEALOUSY

To dream that you are jealous indicates that you may be harboring those same feelings in your waking life. You may also need to look more closely at your self-esteem and see where it is lacking.

JESUS

To dream of Jesus denotes fortitude and consolation during an adversity that will be arising in your life. If you dream that you speak to, pray to, touch, or are touched by Jesus, you will be blessed beyond your imagination: all your dreams will come true.

JEWELRY

To dream of broken jewelry denotes keen disappointment in attaining your highest desires.

JOURNAL

To dream of writing in a journal foretells correspondence from someone you haven't heard from in a while. To dream of reading someone else's journal implies dishonest and disloyal friendships.

JOURNEY

To dream that you go on a journey signifies profit or disappointment, depending on whether the travels are pleasing and successful or whether accidents and disagreeable events intrude.

KEY

To dream of keys in general denotes unexpected changes. If the keys are lost, unpleasant adventures will affect you, and a general sense of losing control of a situation may afflict you. If you are giving them to someone, beware that those around might be trying to steal your power; or you might be too ready to hand over control to something that you should not.

KIDNEY

To dream about your kidneys foretells a serious illness or trouble in your marriage. It indicates a need to cleanse something from your life.

KISSING

To dream that you see children kissing denotes happy reunions in families and satisfactory work. If you dream of kissing your mother or father, you will be very successful in your enterprises and will be honored and beloved by your friends. To kiss a brother or sister suggests much pleasure and good in your association. To kiss your sweetheart in the dark denotes danger and immorality. To kiss her in the light shows that honorable intentions occupy your mind in connection with romance.

KITCHEN

To dream of a kitchen denotes a need for spiritual or emotional nourishment or suggests that this need is being met. To dream that your kitchen is clean and orderly means that your personal life is in order.

KNIFE

To dream of a knife is bad for the dreamer: It portends separation, quarrels, and losses in business affairs. To see rusty knives suggests dissatisfaction and complaints from those in the home, and separation of lovers. A dull knife indicates that hard work is getting you nowhere. Sharp and highly polished knives denote worry. Foes are ever surrounding you. Broken knives speak of defeat, whether in love or business.

LANGUAGES

To dream you hear someone speaking in a foreign language means that you are having a hard time understanding the motives or actions of another.

LAUGHING

To dream that you laugh and feel cheerful predicts success in your undertakings and bright companions socially. Laughing insanely marks disappointment and a lack of harmony in your surroundings.

LAWYER

To dream you are a lawyer when you're not means that you must seek help from another to solve a current dilemma. If you dream you see a lawyer, you will soon be involved in a scandal.

LIAR

If you believe people to be liars in your dream, you may lose faith in a scheme that you have urgently put forward. For someone to call you a liar means that you will experience vexations through deceitful people.

LOTTERY

If you dream of taking great interest in a lottery, you will engage in a worthless enterprise that will cause you to make an unpropitious journey. If you hold the lucky number, you will gain in a speculation that will perplex you and offer much anxiety.

MACARONI

In dreams, eating macaroni represents abundance. To see it in large quantities means that you will save money through the strictest economy.

MADNESS

To dream of being mad reveals trouble ahead for the dreamer and threatens sickness, by which you will lose property.

MANUSCRIPT

To dream that you are writing a manuscript suggests financial gain and notoriety in the near future. To dream of reading another's manuscript implies a small financial loss, but nothing that can't be overcome.

MAP

To dream of a map, or of studying one, suggests that you will contemplate a change in your business. Some disappointing things will occur, but much profit also will follow the change.

MARRIAGE* (WEDDING)

To dream of seeing a marriage denotes enjoyment if the wedding guests attend in pleasing colors and are happy; if they are dressed in black or other somber hues, there will be mourning and sorrow for the dreamer.

MERMAID

If you dream of a mermaid and it is a pleasant dream, you can expect things to go well in the near future. But if it was unpleasant, look for disappointment.

MILK

Cow's milk means good health; goat's milk, business advances. For a farmer, to dream of drinking milk denotes abundant harvest and pleasure in the home; for a traveler, it foretells a fortunate voyage. This is a very propitious dream for women.

MIRROR

To dream of seeing yourself in a mirror indicates that you will face many discouraging issues, and sickness will cause you distress and loss of fortune. It may also foretell unfaithfulness and neglect in marriage. To see another face in the mirror alongside your own indicates that you are leading a double life. You will deceive your friends.

MISCARRIAGE

If you dream of a miscarriage and you are pregnant, this dream has no meaning. If you are single but not pregnant, the dream of a miscarriage foretells of news of a pregnancy or birth, but not necessarily yours. For a married woman, it predicts your own pregnancy. To watch a miscarriage or to know that someone has miscarried in a dream warns of trouble in your family.

MISTLETOE

To dream of mistletoe foretells happiness and great rejoicing. To the young, it predicts many pleasant pastimes. If seen with unpromising signs, however, disappointment will displace pleasure or fortune.

MONEY

To dream of finding money suggests small worries but large happiness. Changes will follow. To pay out money denotes misfortune; to receive gold, great prosperity and unalloyed pleasures. If you lose money, you will experience unhappy hours in the home and affairs will appear gloomy.

MONSTER

To dream of being pursued by a monster indicates that sorrow and misfortune hold prominent places in your immediate future.

MOON

To dream of seeing the moon prognosticates success in love and business affairs. A weird-looking or otherwise altered moon denotes unpropitious romance, domestic infelicities, and disappointing enterprises of a business character. The moon in eclipse implies that contagion will ravage your community.

MORNING

To see the morning dawn clear in your dreams prognosticates the approach of fortune and pleasure.

MOTHER

To see your mother in a dream as she appears in waking life signifies pleasing results from any enterprise. If you engage her in conversation, you will soon have good news from issues you are anxious over.

MUMMY

To dream of a mummy means you will soon help someone find a solution to a problem. If you see yourself as a mummy, you are wrapped up in someone else's problem; you really should walk away from it.

NAKEDNESS

To dream that you are naked betokens monetary luck and improvement in your personal circumstances. If you see others naked, you will uncover deception among friends. To dream that you suddenly discover you nudity and are trying to conceal it denotes you will be socially recognized for a good deed.

NEW YEAR

To dream of the new year signifies prosperity.

NOBEL PRIZE

To dream of receiving this award warns you against arrogance and pride. But if you dream that you are happy that someone else has won it, your personal relationships are heading toward happy times.

NOSE

To see your own nose in a dream indicates force of character and consciousness of your ability to accomplish whatever enterprise you may choose to undertake. If your nose looks smaller than natural, there might be problems in your affairs. Hair growing on your nose indicates extraordinary undertakings that will be carried out by sheer force of character or will. A bleeding nose is prophetic of bad luck.

OCEAN

To dream of a calm ocean, whether sailing on it or not, is always propitious. Dreams of being far out in the ocean and hearing the waves forebodes problems in business life and quarrels and stormy periods in the household.

OCTOPUS

To dream of this sea animal suggests that movement is afoot in your personal life or career. To dream that you are caught up in its tentacles warns you against using others to further your career.

ORANGE (FRUIT)

Seeing orange trees or eating oranges in a dream signifies health and prosperous surroundings.

ORCHARD

Dreaming of passing through blossoming orchards with your sweetheart heralds the delightful consummation of a long courtship. If the orchard is filled with ripening fruit, it denotes recompense for faithful service to those who serve under masters, and full fruition of designs for the leaders of enterprises.

ORGAN

To hear the pealing of a pipe organ signifies lasting friendships and wellestablished fortune. If you dream of rendering harmonious music on an organ, you will be fortunate along your path to worldly comfort, and much social distinction will be given you.

ORPHAN

Dreaming of orphans means that the unhappy cares of others will touch your sympathies; sacrificing your own enjoyment will bring you joy. If the orphans are related to you, new duties will come into your life, causing estrangement from friends.

PANIC

If you dream that you panic, you will find much peace of mind and calmness surrounding you and your family now. To dream of others panicking while you stay calm means that you will have to deal with a family problem that you wanted to stay out of.

PARENTS

To see your parents looking cheerful in your dream suggests harmony and pleasant associates. If your parents appear to you after they are dead, it is a message of love and warmth, and sometimes a warning. You should be careful in your dealings

PEBBLES

In dreams, pebbles and small stones represent minor troubles and vexations in your life. To be throwing them, or to have them thrown at you, indicates that you are being over-sensitive; minor criticisms tend to wound you.

PHD

To dream of receiving this degree means advancement in your career. Giving one to someone else suggests a possible job loss.

PILL

To dream that you take pills indicates that you will have responsibilities to look after, but they will bring you much comfort and enjoyment. To give pills to others signifies that you will be criticized for being disagreeable.

PIMPLE

To dream of your flesh being full of pimples denotes worry over trifles. To see others pimpled signifies that you will be troubled by illness and complaints from others.

PITCHFORK

Pitchforks in dreams represent struggles for betterment of fortune and some sort of great mental or physical labor.

PLAGUE

To dream of a plague denotes disappointing returns in business. If you are afflicted with the plague, you will keep your business in the black with the greatest maneuvering. If you are trying to escape a plague, some trouble that looks overwhelming is pursuing you.

POETRY

To dream of poetry betokens an interesting and unusual new friend.

PRAISE

To dream of receiving praise foretells an unexpected gift of money. To dream of giving praise forewarns of an unanticipated expense.

PRAYER

To dream of saying prayers foretells peace of mind and happiness in life. To hear others pray suggests loyal and lasting friendships.

PRIEST

A dream of a priest is an augury of ill, indicating the need for spiritual advice or guidance in your life.

PRINCE, PRINCESS

To dream of being this member of the royal family suggests an advancement in your social status; but this could be surrounded by jealousy, so you need to watch your back.

PROPHET

To dream of a prophet means you will have great blessings in your future and will enjoy an expanded spiritual base.

PURGATORY

To dream of purgatory means you will soon have to make a decision. You might not initially believe it is the right thing for you, but it will turn out to be a blessing.

QUARANTINE

To dream of being quarantined means that you will be placed in a disagreeable position by the malicious intriguing of enemies.

QUARREL

Quarrels in dreams portend unhappiness and fierce altercations. To a young woman, quarrels are the signal of unpleasantness fatal to a relationship, and to a married woman they bring separation or ongoing disagreement. To hear others quarreling denotes unsatisfactory business and disappointing trade.

QUARRY

To dream of being in a quarry and seeing the workmen busy suggests that you will advance by hard labor.

QUICKSAND

If you find yourself in quicksand while dreaming, you will meet with loss and deceit. If you are unable to get out of the quicksand, you will be involved in overwhelming misfortune.

RABBI

To dream of this Jewish scholar, regardless of your personal faith, suggests that things are going your way. But if you are Jewish and dream of a rabbi, it signifies prosperity through hard work.

RAIN

To dream of being out in a clear shower of rain suggests that you enjoy pleasure with the zest of youth, and prosperity will come to you. If the rain descends from dark clouds, you will feel alarmed over the gravity of your undertakings.

RAINBOW

To see a rainbow in a dream prognosticates unusual events. Affairs will assume a more promising aspect. To see the rainbow hanging low over green trees signifies unconditional success in any undertaking.

REAPER

To dream of seeing harvesters busy at work denotes prosperity and contentment. If they appear to be going through dried stubble, crops will be poor and business will fall off. To see idle reapers implies that something discouraging will occur in the midst of prosperity.

RED

To dream of this color or of any article that stands out because it is red indicates great passion and sensitivity in your emotional relationships.

RELIGION

If you dream of discussing religion and you feel religiously inclined, you will find much to mar the calmness of your life, and business will turn disagreeable for you. If you judge yourself in the midst of religious rapture, you may almost be induced to give up your own personality to please someone whom you hold in reverent esteem.

REPUBLICAN

To dream of being a Republican when you are not means you will be seeking advice from someone you never thought you would.

RESURRECTION

If you dream that you are resurrected from the dead, you will have some great vexation but will eventually gain your desires.

REVENGE

To dream of taking revenge is a sign of a weak and uncharitable nature, which, if not properly governed, will bring you troubles and loss of friends. If others avenge themselves on you, you will have much to fear from enemies.

RIDDLES

To dream that you are trying to solve riddles means you will engage in something that will try your patience and involve a great deal of your money.

ROOT CANAL

If you dream of this dental procedure, expect health concerns to arise soon.

ROSE

To dream of seeing roses blooming and fragrant suggests that a joyful occasion is nearing, and you will possess the faithful love of your sweetheart. Withered roses signify the absence of loved ones. White roses, if seen without sunshine or dew, denote serious if not fatal illness.

SADNESS

To dream of being sad means you will soon find that your troubles are over.

SAINT

To dream of a saint suggests unusual blessings and difficulties being overcome.

SALARY

If you dream you are not being given a salary increase, you are likely to see financial gain through an unexpected source. If you request a raise and it is granted in your dream, this portends a monetary loss. Paying a salary to someone foretells unexpected good luck with money.

SALT

Salt is an omen of discordant surroundings when seen in dreams. You will usually find after dreaming of salt that everything goes awry, and quarrels and dissatisfaction show themselves in the family circle.

SAND

To dream of sand is indicative of losses.

SATAN

To dream of Satan predicts dangerous adventures; you will be forced to use strategy to keep up honorable appearances. To dream that you kill him suggests that you desert wicked or immoral companions to live upon a higher plane. If he comes to you under the guise of literature, you are warned against promiscuous friendships, and especially flatterers. If he comes in the shape of wealth or power, you will fail to use your influence for harmony or for the elevation of others. If he takes the form of music, you are likely to succumb to his wiles.

SCAFFOLD

To dream of a scaffold suggests keen disappointment in failing to secure the object of your affection. If you ascend a scaffold, you will be misunderstood and censured by your friends for an action that you never committed. To descend one predicts that you will be guilty of wrongdoing and will suffer the penalty.

SCHOOL

To dream of attending school indicates distinction in literary work. If you are young and at school in the dream, you will find that sorrow and reverses will make you sincerely long for the simple trust and pleasures of days of yore.

SCREAMING

To dream of other people screaming suggests distressing news. To dream you are screaming is a good omen for all that concerns you.

SERVANT

To dream of a servant is a sign that you will have good fortune, despite gloomy appearances. Anger is likely to push you into unnecessary worry and quarrels. To discharge a servant foretells regret and loss. To quarrel with one in your dream indicates that you will, upon waking, have real cause for censuring someone derelict in duty. To be robbed by one shows that you have someone near you who does not respect the laws of ownership.

SEX

To dream of changing your sex implies honor and success in family matters. To dream of sexually teasing someone, or of being teased, means that a goal you are working toward will prove unworthy.

SHARK

To dream of sharks suggests formidable enemies. To see a shark pursuing and attacking you denotes that unavoidable reverses will sink you into despondency and foreboding. If you see sharks sporting in clear water, jealousy is secretly but surely bringing you disquiet and misfortune while you bask in the sunshine. Dreaming of a dead shark implies reconciliation and renewed prosperity.

SHOOTING

To dream that you see or hear shooting signifies unhappiness between married couples and sweethearts because of selfishness; it also bodes dissatisfaction in business and other projects due to negligence. To dream that you are shot and are feeling the sensations of dying denotes that you may meet unexpected abuse from the ill feelings of friends; if you escape death by waking up, you will be fully reconciled with them later on.

SINGLE

For married people to dream that they are single foretells that their union may not be harmonious. It could also indicate that they need to find a spirit of independence in their union.

SOUL

To dream of seeing your soul leaving your body signifies that you are in danger of sacrificing yourself to useless designs, which will dwarf your sense of honor and cause you pain.

SPIDER

To dream of a spider suggests that you will be careful and energetic in your labors, and your fortune will be amassed to pleasing proportions. To see one building its web foretells that you will be happy and secure in your own home. To kill one signifies quarrels. If one bites you, you will be the victim of unfaithfulness and will suffer from enemies in your business.

STOMACH

To dream of having pain in your stomach signifies good health. If you dream that you have a fat stomach and you do not, you need to see a doctor.

STRENGTH

To dream of being very strong means you are aiming too high in an ambition or goal. If you watch someone showing off strength in a dream, a passionate love affair will turn ugly.

SUFFOCATING

To dream that you are suffocating suggests that you will experience deep sorrow and mortification as a result of the conduct of someone you love. Be careful of your health after this dream.

SUICIDE

To commit suicide in a dream indicates that misfortune will hang heavily over you.

SUN

To dream of seeing a clear, shining sunrise foretells joyous events and prosperity, which give delightful promise. To see the sun at midday denotes the maturity of ambition and indicates unbounded satisfaction.

SWORD

To dream that you wear a sword indicates that you will fill some public position with honor. To have your sword taken from you denotes your vanquishment in rivalry.

TEARS

To dream that you are in tears indicates that an affliction will soon envelop you. If you see others shedding tears, your sorrows will affect the happiness of others.

TEETH

An ordinary dream of teeth augurs an unpleasant contact with sickness or disquieting people. If you dream that your teeth are loose, expect failures and gloomy tidings. If the doctor pulls your tooth, you will endure a desperate illness; if not fatal, it will be lingering.

TERROR

To dream that you feel terror about any object or event indicates that disappointment and loss will envelop you. To see others in terror means that the unhappiness of friends will seriously affect you.

TEXT MESSAGE

To dream of sending or receiving text messages on your cell phone means you will soon be hearing from an old friend or acquaintance.

THUNDER

To dream of hearing thunder indicates that you may be threatened with reverses in your business. If you are in a thundershower, trouble and grief are close to you. To hear terrific peals of thunder that make the earth quake portends great loss and disappointment.

TIDAL WAVE

To dream of a tidal wave that is free of debris portends an amazing career and personal change that will be very beneficial to you. If the water is dirty and carrying debris, it warns of hard times ahead.

TIGER

If you dream of a tiger advancing toward you, you will be tormented and persecuted by enemies. If it attacks you, failure will bury you in gloom. If you succeed in warding it off or killing it, you will be extremely successful in all your undertakings.

TONGUE

To dream of seeing your own tongue suggests that you will be looked upon with disfavor by your acquaintances. If you see the tongue of another, scandal may vilify you. To dream that your tongue is affected in any way means that your carelessness in talking will get you into trouble.

UFO

Dreaming of a UFO suggests that profound spiritual change is coming.

UGLINESS

To dream that you are ugly denotes that you will have a difficulty with your sweetheart, and your prospects will suffer.

UNICORN

A dream of this mythical creature betokens a period of beneficial change.

VALENTINE

To dream that you are sending valentines foretells that you will lose opportunities to enrich yourself.

VAMPIRE

To dream of vampires warns that you need to be more serious and responsible.

VIRGIN

To dream of a virgin foretells comparative luck in your speculations.

VOICES

To dream of hearing calm and pleasing voices denotes pleasant reconciliations; high-pitched and angry voices signify disappointments and unfavorable situations. To hear weeping voices shows that sudden anger will cause you to inflict injury on a friend.

VOMITING

To dream of vomiting is a sign that you will be afflicted with a malady that threatens invalidism, or that you will be connected with a racy scandal.

WAKE

To dream that you attend a wake suggests that you will sacrifice an important engagement to enjoy an ill-favored assignation.

WAR

To dream of war foretells unfortunate conditions in business, and much disorder and strife in domestic affairs. For a young woman to dream that her lover goes to war indicates that she will hear of something detrimental to her lover's character.

WARTS

If you are troubled with warts on your person in your dreams, you will be unable to successfully parry the thrusts made at your honor. To see warts leaving your hands foretells that you will overcome disagreeable obstructions to fortune.

WEDDING RING

To dream that a wedding ring is bright and shiny suggests that you will be shielded from cares and infidelity.

WILL

To dream that you are making your will foretells momentous trials and tribulations. If you dream that a will is against your interests, you may have disputes and disorderly proceedings to combat in some event soon to transpire. If you fail to prove a will's validity, you are in danger of libelous slander.

WIDOW

To dream that you are a widow indicates that you will have many troubles through malicious people. If a man dreams that he marries a widow, he may see some cherished undertaking crumble in disappointment.

ZIPPER

This portends social problems if a zipper is broken or stuck. But to dream of a zipper that fastens easily augurs satisfaction in your social life.